A HIGHER DIMENSION

RYAN LeSTRANGE

CHARISMA
HOUSE

Copyright © 2019 by Ryan LeStrange
All rights reserved

Visit the author's website at RyanLeStrange.com.

Library of Congress Cataloging-in-Publication Data:
An application to register this book for cataloging has been submitted to the Library of Congress.

International Standard Book Number: 978-1-62999-703-2
E-book ISBN: 978-1-62999-705-6

19 20 21 22 23 — 987654321
Printed in the United States of America

CONTENTS

Chapter 1

DIMENSIONS AND REALMS

As I have studied some of the most breathtaking miracles of the Bible, it has become clear to me that they were often the result of another realm being manifested in the earth. Those who represent the kingdom of God act in an official capacity as fully authorized ambassadors of the King in all His glory. Wherever they go, a supernatural zone of power and glory transforms the space around them.

> Then they went forth and preached everywhere, the Lord working with them and confirming the word through the accompanying signs. Amen.
> —MARK 16:20, MEV

Jesus had fully commissioned the burgeoning New Testament church with the weight of the kingdom. His followers went about demonstrating the power of the kingdom. They were functioning from a higher dimension.

TRANSFORMING YOUR TERRITORY

The great healing ministry of John G. Lake shook his generation. It also shook the city of Spokane, Washington, through the ministries of the Healing Rooms, which Lake created upon his return from South Africa. After Lake opened up the Healing Rooms, Spokane became recognized by the secular community as the healthiest city in America.[1]

In Lake's own words, "It became easy for me to detach myself from the course of life, so that while my hands and mind were engaged in the common affairs of every day, my spirit maintained its attitude of communion with God."[2] Lake had both the faith and the glory to transform a territory! He was carrying something from another space and invading the powers of hell with the glory of heaven.

A NEW DIMENSION

A dimension is not a time but a space, a location. Our life on earth is marked and measured by times and seasons. God provides insight and wisdom concerning the prophetic season that we are in! Rightly discerning the times is a prophetic gift, but a dimension is something altogether different. It is a space, a place, and a location!

When we were born again, we were born not into a season but into a dimension.

> Jesus answered, "Truly, truly, I say to you, unless one is born of water and the Spirit he cannot enter into the kingdom of God."
>
> —John 3:5

The Bible speaks of the kingdom as a realm, a place, a reality, not as a time. In this scripture, entry is not speaking about a time or a season but a place. Through the gateway of salvation we move into the space of the kingdom. As we come into proper understanding of the weight and reality of the kingdom, we are able to subdue the forces of hell at work in the earth realm.

> For He rescued us from the domain of darkness, and transferred us to the kingdom of His beloved Son, in whom we have redemption, the forgiveness of sins.
>
> —Colossians 1:13–14

We have been translated or transferred from one place to another. We have been relocated from one realm to another. We have moved from one dimension to another. Jesus, through His sacrifice at the cross, paid our debts fully and transferred us from the domain—the rulership and authority—of darkness into His marvelous power and rule! We are now fully active citizens of the kingdom, called to dwell in a new dimension.

> And you were dead in your trespasses and sins, in which you formerly walked according to the course of this world, according to the prince of the power of the air, of the spirit that is now working in the sons of disobedience. Among them we too all formerly lived in the lusts of our flesh, indulging the desires of the flesh and of the mind, and were by nature children of wrath, even as the rest. But God, being rich in mercy, because of His great love with which He loved us, even when we were dead in our transgressions, made us alive together with Christ (by grace you have been saved), and raised us up with Him, and seated us with Him in the heavenly places in Christ Jesus, so that in the ages to come He might show the surpassing riches of His grace in kindness toward us in Christ Jesus.
> —EPHESIANS 2:1–7

In verse 6 of this passage the word *heavenly* is the Greek word *epouranios*, which means "heavenly, celestial, in the heavenly sphere, the sphere of spiritual activities; met: divine, spiritual."[3] *Places* in this context means in, on, or among. Again, it denotes a location. The picture is that we have been removed from the kingdom, or place, of darkness and brought into the space, or place, of the kingdom of God. Again, this is speaking of a realm, not a time or season.

A HEAVENLY MINDSET

> Therefore if you have been raised up with Christ, keep seeking the things above, where Christ is, seated at the right hand of God. Set your mind on the things above, not on the things that are on earth. For you have died and your life is hidden with Christ in God.
>
> —COLOSSIANS 3:1–3

The Bible declares that Christ is at the right hand of God. This is a location, a destination inside of the heavenly dimension. We are told to put our minds on the things in that dimension. This instruction contains a power key! Meditating on the reality of the kingdom as well as Christ's position in the kingdom and our existence in Him taps realms of power and glory.

Meditation creates access points. This is true in both the good and the bad sense. For example, when we meditate upon defeat, fear, or bondage, we become overwhelmed by negative emotions, unclean atmospheres, and demonic plans. Our inner thought life guides our decisions, our emotions, and the trajectory of our lives.

> Finally, brethren, whatever is true, whatever is honorable, whatever is right, whatever is pure, whatever is lovely, whatever is of good repute, if there is any excellence and if anything worthy of praise, dwell on these things.
>
> —PHILIPPIANS 4:8

We often miss the benefit, blessing, and power of heavenly spheres because our minds are much too earthly. Perhaps you have heard someone say, "You are so heavenly minded that you are of no earthly good." This statement is often expressed referring to those who seem ineffective in natural living and assignments. But it facilitates a lie. A truly heavenly minded person is extremely powerful.

John G. Lake said, "That is only one of the living facts of what Christianity is: the divine power of Jesus Christ by the Holy Spirit, filling a man's soul and body, flashing through his nature like holy flame, accomplishing the will of God."[4]

Chapter 2

PROPHETIC REALMS

As PROPHETIC PEOPLE we see, hear, and know. It is our portion to be invited into the mysteries and secrets of God. We have been created to know things, we have been created to see things, and we have been created to operate in another dimension of revelation and insight.

In his book *Dreaming With God*, Bill Johnson writes:

> But there's another part to this equation—*"it's the glory of kings to search out a matter"* [Prov. 25:2]! We are kings and priests to our God (see Rev. 1:6). Our royal identity never shines brighter than when we pursue hidden things with the confidence that we have legal access to such things. Mysteries are our inheritance. Our kingship, our role in ruling and reigning with Christ, comes to the forefront when we seek Him for answers to the dilemmas of the world around us....It is important to note, ruling from God's perspective means to be the servant of all. Too many have embraced this theology, and have used it as an excuse to pursue ruling

over others in the way Jesus warned against. Our strong suit has been, and always will be, serving.[1]

TIMES AND SEASONS

Prophets and prophetic people release prophetic words, revelations, and decrees. Prophetic words are often connected with times and seasons. These words often deal with *chronos*, the natural passing of time, or *kairos*, times pregnant with potential. Part of the prophetic vocabulary is the proper understanding and informing of the times.

> Then Elisha said, "Listen to the word of the LORD; thus says the LORD, 'Tomorrow about this time a measure of fine flour will be sold for a shekel, and two measures of barley for a shekel, in the gate of Samaria.'"
>
> The royal officer on whose hand the king was leaning answered the man of God and said, "Behold, if the LORD should make windows in heaven, could this thing be?" Then he said, "Behold, you will see it with your own eyes, but you will not eat of it."
>
> —2 KINGS 7:1–2

There are two types of prophetic words related to times and seasons: foretelling and forth-telling. Foretelling prophetic words are declarations of future events. This realm of the prophetic releases revelation of that which is to come. To give a forth-telling prophetic word, on the other hand, is to declare and to utter forth, to release a divine revelation or declare divine will, to interpret the mysteries of heaven, to make known the will of God and the heart of God—the agenda of heaven.

There is prophetic wisdom and a mantle of accuracy for times and seasons. Prophets decree the assignment and mandate of the Lord for specific times and seasons. Prophets identify the plan of God in a space of time. Prophets reveal the heart of God in a time and season. These words are key because they arm us for effective kingdom function within a time and season.

> Of the sons of Issachar, men who understood the times, with knowledge of what Israel should do, their chiefs were two hundred; and all their kinsmen were at their command.
>
> —1 Chronicles 12:32

There is revelation for times and seasons. There is anointing for times and seasons. There is function for times and seasons. There is a flow for times and seasons.

To properly discern the time, one must ask: What is the forth-telling word? What is the heart of God, the mind of God, for *right now*? What is God doing? What does God desire to do? How is He leading His people?

What is the foretelling word? What is happening in world affairs? What is happening in my life? What is the word of the Lord to the prophets for this time?

THE SPIRIT OF PROPHECY AND THE OFFICE OF THE PROPHET

Every believer has the distinct privilege of being able to be led by the Spirit of God (Rom. 8:14). There are a variety of ways that God can bring insight and illumination to a believer in order to reveal His will. All of these various methods of communication are found in the prophetic realm.

There is a difference between functioning in the prophetic realm (hearing, seeing, and knowing) through the spirit or gift of prophecy and being commissioned by God to the office of the prophet.

+ **The spirit of prophecy, the gift of prophecy, and the leading of the Spirit**: This is available in the believer's ministry. This is part of the rivers flowing in our belly. This is the Romans 8 anointing—to know!

+ **The office of the prophet**: The office of the prophet connects the *ekklesia*—the church—to the plans and purposes of the Lord for any given time. Multiple layers and levels of the office of the prophet should be in operation in the ekklesia, such as prophetic preaching, prophetic worship, minstrels, prophetic words, and prophetic decrees.

He has made us to be a kingdom, priests to His God and Father—to Him be the glory and the dominion forever and ever. Amen.

—Revelation 1:6

It is important to note that the office of the prophet carries a governmental authority for the ekklesia that the gift of prophecy does not. Prophets are a part of the governmental arm of the church. Believers who prophesy and are led by the Spirit of God do not have the same governmental mandate and authority as prophets do. As priests and kings we can minister to the Lord and know His will for our lives. We are anointed to see and hear for our homes, our families, and our businesses. However, our status as believers does not mean we are anointed to govern the ekklesia; this is a different rank and office. The simple gift of prophecy starts to misfire when believers try to fulfill the office of the prophet without the spiritual authority and anointing to do so.

UNDERSTANDING THE TIMES

Seasons are vitally important. Properly understanding and responding to times and seasons is critical. But there is more...

Seasons exist within dimensions! Dimensions do not exist within seasons.

Let me provide an example: Colorado is a destination. Winter in the Rockies is a season. *The season is contained in the dimension.*

When we understand the principle of dimensions, we can fully navigate and access the power that is available to us. Seasons are contained within dimensions. The kingdom has different seasons, each filled with unique potential and purpose that must be unlocked through prophetic understanding and radical obedience.

Chapter 3

THE POWER OF IMPARTATION

THE APOSTLE PAUL wrote, "For I long to see you so that I may impart some spiritual gift to you, that you may be established" (Rom. 1:11). Impartation can shift a life, accelerate a calling, and heal a body. Impartation releases the substance of heaven on a person. To impart, one must have a resident anointing and power. A person who is empty holds no power to impart. A place that is void of anointing and life has nothing to pour out. Impartation is an apostolic characteristic. It is part of the sending.

You are sent and empowered. Believers must learn to discern people and places that have the anointing and then make a demand upon that anointing. The anointing destroys the yokes, heals disease, and brings life! Let's examine two different levels of impartation.

ATMOSPHERIC IMPARTATION

There is a dimension of impartation where atmospheres become infused with the power and glory of God—when you come into contact with the very atmosphere, you are changed! I believe we need to contend for this more and more. We need to capture the power and glory of God in such a tangible way that people are immediately touched and empowered.

Two examples of atmospheric impartation in the Word are Peter's shadow and Paul's prayer cloths. In Acts 19:11–12 we read that Paul had so fully realized the dimension of the kingdom that his presence manifested the ability to break demonic powers and release the weight of heaven. Men of God took cloths from his meetings and laid them upon the tormented and afflicted. The anointing flowed while the impartation of the kingdom of light destroyed the operation of the kingdom of darkness.

Acts 5:14–15 tells us that Peter got so far into dimensions of glory that his shadow healed the sick! There was no power in the shadow, but if you got close enough to Peter, you became overwhelmed by the kingdom. The kingdom of God came crashing over your sickness and disease.

These men lived and moved in the kingdom. They were able to create places and spaces of impartation. I believe this is something that God wants to manifest now in this generation. He is looking for people who will realize the fullness of His kingdom and move in His power. He is looking for people who will dare to believe for higher dimensions of kingdom living and function. He is looking for places that will host His glory and manifest His power. Accessing and creating open dimensions of glory unlocks divine power.

God invites new creation living! We are called to live in the reality of new creation truth and power.

> Therefore if anyone is in Christ [that is, grafted in, joined to Him by faith in Him as Savior], he is a new creature [reborn and renewed by the Holy Spirit]; the old things [the previous moral and spiritual condition] have passed away. Behold, new things have come [because spiritual awakening brings a new life]. But all these things are from God, who reconciled us to Himself through Christ [making us acceptable to Him] and gave us the ministry of reconciliation [so that by our example we might bring others to Him].
>
> —2 Corinthians 5:17–18, amp

In Christ we are glory carriers, those who manifest the kingdom. We carry the mantle of *manifestation*—to show forth or make visible the King, the kingdom, and the glory! Through atmospheric impartation the space surrounding us becomes infused with heaven.

Sonship Impartation

This is also a position, a location—not a season or a set time. Through this impartation you occupy your place as a son or daughter of the Most High God. It is a reality that you can freely move from that place into the power and glory of God because it is your birthright. This is the kingdom in action. This is the glory of God in manifestation.

These realms exist and are waiting to be discovered by God's people. They must be discovered, acted upon, and accepted by faith. When you fully embrace this truth, you become established! You no longer move in and out of power; you dwell in the realm of power and majesty.

> As for you, the anointing which you received from Him abides in you, and you have no need for anyone to teach you; but as His anointing teaches you about all things, and is true and is not a lie, and just as it has taught you, you abide in Him.
> —1 John 2:27

This verse decrees an abiding anointing. It does not speak of a season but a continual reality. It speaks of a resident anointing, a heavenly power available to us as sons and daughters of God.

Chapter 4

APOSTLES ARE UNLOCKERS

*Then I will set the key of the house of David
on his shoulder, when he opens no one
will shut, when he shuts no one will open.*
—Isaiah 22:22

Apostles assist the ekklesia in accessing dimensions and realms in the spirit. Part of their forerunner DNA is to open up spiritual territories. Once you access a realm, you have *full* availability of everything in that realm.

The apostolic mantle causes men and women to pioneer the opening of realms to shake their generations. This is the gift of apostolic weight and anointing. Smith Wigglesworth plowed open the dead-raising anointing in his time. John G. Lake pioneered the revelation of the spirit of life and the healing mysteries of God in his generation. William Seymour restored Pentecost to the modern church. Lester Sumrall challenged demonic powers and mantled a generation with authority. Kenneth Hagin taught the church to believe in God again. Aimee Semple McPherson blazed the trail to a move of signs, wonders, and miracles in her day. She became the founder of a denomination in a day when many believed that women were not called to preach.

Each of these pioneers bucked the trends of his or her day to establish something unique, powerful, and kingdom initiated. They were not building off popular ideas or carnal church trends. Their spirits had been touched by the living God! They had been mantled from another realm.

The list continues today! God creates men and women with an unusual appetite for the kingdom, and they explore places in God that most never know. Then they are released to touch and mantle their generation. They open up levels in the Spirit that those before them have not opened. They navigate and experience dimensions of the kingdom to properly steward the truths and the power of God in their day.

UNLOCKING NEW REALMS

Before we can access a realm, we must both discover and pursue it. First, God opens our eyes to see the realm. This is the prophetic nature, to hear and see. Then pursuit is unlocked, and God challenges us to press in to the revealed realm. Finally, we access the realm by faith, by decree, and by meditation.

Apostolic leaders should pioneer the exploration of realms through prayer, revelation, vision casting, and pursuit.

Different realms require different types of pursuit.

- You access by revelation.
- You access by faith.
- You access by authority.
- You access by engaging the climate and culture of that realm.
    - There is a climate and culture of healing.
    - There is a climate and culture of glory.
    - There is a climate and culture of fire.

Realms have sounds—creating the sounds of a realm can open it up. Learn the sound and expression of the realms of God. This is why the ministry of *nabi* prophets is vital; they bubble forth the words and language of realms.

Prophetic worship creates and builds the atmosphere of a realm. Apostles are given language to articulate the reality and existence of realms. They invite the kingdom citizens to occupy those realms. The apostolic anointing is a governmental anointing. Apostles govern and steward realms.

+ Apostolic people pray governing prayers.

+ Apostolic people worship with songs and sounds that subdue territories and break open realms.

+ Apostolic people move in uncommon faith.

+ Apostolic people move in uncommon revelation.

+ Apostolic people move in uncommon authority.

+ Apostolic people occupy uncommon realms and dimensions.

Chapter 5

THE GLORY REALM

Then Moses said, "I pray You,
show me Your glory!"
—Exodus 33:18

T HE WORD FOR *glory* here is *kabod*, meaning heaviness, heavy presence, heavy glory—the weighty realms of God's spirit.

Glory is the atmosphere (the space) around the throne. The call to glory is a mantle of proximity. Walking in glory requires abundant revelation of the nearness of God.

I love the glory realm! The sweet incense of intimacy is experienced in the glory realm. The fragrance of God's presence is manifest in the glory realm. Angels dwell in the glory realm. Unusual, shocking things take place in the glory realm.

THE CLOUD AND THE FIRE

Authentic glory does not just give you an unusual experience; it brings unusual freedom to your life.

> Then He brought them out with silver and gold, and among His tribes there was not one who stumbled. Egypt was glad when they departed, for the dread of them had fallen upon them. He spread a cloud for a covering, and fire to illumine by night. They asked, and He brought quail, and satisfied them with the bread of heaven. He opened the rock and water flowed out; it ran in the dry places like a river. For He remembered His holy word with Abraham His servant; and He brought forth His people with joy, His chosen ones with a joyful shout. He gave them also the lands of the nations, that they might take possession of the fruit of the peoples' labor, so that they might keep His statutes and observe His laws.
>
> —PSALM 105:37–45

This is one of my favorite glory passages in the Bible. God led His kids out of slavery and bondage with a cloud and fire. This realm of authentic glory brings forth uncommon deliverance. As the glory of God enters a space, demonic bondages fall like a stack of dominoes. This is the picture of what God does in the glory realm.

In the glory realm they were led out! There are people rising in the glory realm who will follow the cloud and fire to bring their generation out of bondage, disease, fear, and darkness, and into the glory of God.

In the glory the people of Israel found supernatural health and life. Miracles and healing are common in the glory realm. There was also provision and financial miracles; Israel was loaded down with silver and gold! The glory will bring economy into your life. The glory cloud covered them, and the fire led them. We need both the fire and the glory. We need the cloud of God's peace and presence, but we also need the burning fire that purifies us and baptizes us. Glory is multifaceted! Go for uncommon and unusual realms of glory.

RELEASING THE REALMS OF GLORY

Glory overrides the report of man and releases the authority of heaven. Glory does not just bend natural law; it defies it! Tumors disappear in the glory. Cells are literally changed in the glory. When you enter the glory, you exit the limitations of earth!

We are not called just to seek the glory; we are called to carry and release the glory. The glory is a part of who we are. We are glory carriers. Where we go, the glory of God goes! As Ruth Ward Heflin wrote in her book *Revival Glory*, "When you discover things that seem to contribute to the glory, do those things more; and when you find things that seem to diminish the glory, stop doing them. It's as simple as that."[1]

> For the earth will be filled with the knowledge of
> the glory of the LORD, as the waters cover the sea.
> —Habakkuk 2:14

God wants to cover the whole earth with His glory! He wants the glory to reign over the nations. Our job description is to uncover, unlock, explore, and release the realms of glory. We are called to teach nations about glory. We are called to lead people into glory. We are called to bring people out of bondage and into glory.

Minister and author Joshua Mills speaks of a glory cloud:

> And that's why when the glory cloud shows up and it comes in your homes, when it comes in a meeting like this, when you think you have come into a realization of the glory working in your life, it's suddenly you feel like you are at home. Suddenly you begin to know what you've always known. You begin to know what you've always known because it's spirit calling unto spirit, deep calling unto deep, and finally you realize: "This is what I was created for. This is what I was made for. This is my home. This is my place. This is my destiny. This is what God has purposed me for." God is wanting to put each of us in the glory cloud of His presence. God is wanting you to offer the

high praise because the higher praise will always take you into the higher place, and God has called you to live in the higher place. Ha. We just offer God the bottom of the barrel, all kinds of bargain praise, and then we wonder why we are getting the bargain basement kind of miracles. They're not bad, but they are what they are. God has told you the greatest things. God has told you that you have the greater glory released in your life.[2]

The glory is in us! It is part of our new nature. We are called to manifest the glory.

Therefore having such a hope, we use great boldness in our speech, and are not like Moses, who used to put a veil over his face so that the sons of Israel would not look intently at the end of what was fading away. But their minds were hardened; for until this very day at the reading of the old covenant the same veil remains unlifted, because it is removed in Christ. But to this day whenever Moses is read, a veil lies over their heart; but whenever a person turns to the Lord, the veil is taken away. Now the Lord is the Spirit, and where the Spirit of the Lord is, there is liberty. But we all, with unveiled face, beholding as in a mirror the glory of the Lord, are being transformed into the

> same image from glory to glory, just as from the
> Lord, the Spirit.
>
> —2 Corinthians 3:12–18

As manifest sons of God, glory is our inheritance! We should decree glory. Expect glory, and pray for more revelation of the glory.

> Then the cloud covered the tent of meeting, and the glory of the Lord filled the tabernacle. Moses was not able to enter the tent of meeting because the cloud had settled on it, and the glory of the Lord filled the tabernacle.
>
> —Exodus 40:34–35

> Then Moses went up with Aaron, Nadab and Abihu, and seventy of the elders of Israel, and they saw the God of Israel; and under His feet there appeared to be a pavement of sapphire, as clear as the sky itself.
>
> —Exodus 24:9–10

God spoke to Moses from the midst of the cloud of glory! This is what God desires to do in our day. He wants to speak to kingdom leaders from the midst of the cloud. He wants to bring them into glory realms so they carry the breath of the glory to the people of God. He wants to bring them forth as ambassadors of the glory.

The angel answered and said to her, "The Holy Spirit will come upon you, and the power of the Most High will overshadow you; and for that reason the holy Child shall be called the Son of God."

—LUKE 1:35

Jesus was conceived in glory! The Hebrew word here for *overshadow* was often used in connection with the cloud in the Old Testament. The cloud would overshadow.

"The latter glory of this house will be greater than the former," says the LORD of hosts, "and in this place I will give peace," declares the LORD of hosts.

—HAGGAI 2:9

God is the glory in the midst of His people!

"For I," declares the LORD, "will be a wall of fire around her, and I will be the glory in her midst."

—ZECHARIAH 2:5

Jesus was received up in the cloud!

And after He had said these things, He was lifted up while they were looking on, and a cloud received Him out of their sight.

—ACTS 1:9

Jesus was conceived and sent into the world in glory, and then the Father received Him back to heaven in glory. Wherever you find Jesus, you find the glory. If we have been with Jesus, then we have been in the glory realm. We will manifest the glory of God. We will manifest the fire of God. We will manifest the cloud of His presence.

Chapter 6

THE MIRACLE REALM

THERE IS A dimension where the supernatural becomes natural. There is a dimension where sudden manifestations of the kingdom and power of God break forth.

There is a miracle dimension. In this space natural law is subjected to the law and authority of God. In this dimension blind eyes open. In this dimension crooked limbs are made straight. In this dimension bondage falls away. In this dimension financial turnarounds happen suddenly.

The disciples were charged to minister from the dimension of the miraculous. As ambassadors of the kingdom they were instructed not just to articulate but also to demonstrate:

> These twelve Jesus sent out after instructing them: "Do not go in the way of the Gentiles, and do not enter any city of the Samaritans; but rather go to the lost sheep of the house of Israel. And as you go, preach, saying, 'The kingdom of heaven is at hand.' Heal the sick, raise the dead, cleanse the

lepers, cast out demons. Freely you received, freely give."

—MATTHEW 10:5–8

Ministering from the position of kingdom jurisdiction and authority releases a strong flow of the miraculous. When we know who we are, we are able to manifest the power of God. Miracles are connected to identity.

THE PROPHETIC ANOINTING AND THE SPIRIT OF FAITH

In the Book of Mark we find the story of Jesus miraculously healing the daughter of a man named Jairus:

> They came to the house of the synagogue official; and He saw a commotion, and people loudly weeping and wailing. And entering in, He said to them, "Why make a commotion and weep? The child has not died, but is asleep." They began laughing at Him. But putting them all out, He took along the child's father and mother and His own companions, and entered the room where the child was. Taking the child by the hand, He said to her, "Talitha kum!" (which translated means, "Little girl, I say to you, get up!"). Immediately the girl got up and began to walk, for she was twelve years old. And immediately they were completely

astounded. And He gave them strict orders that no one should know about this, and He said that something should be given her to eat.

—MARK 5:38–43

When Jesus addressed Jairus' daughter, He saw the girl as asleep, not dead. We know that in the natural realm the girl was dead. So what was taking place here? What was Jesus doing? How was Jesus moving? What was Jesus thinking?

I believe Jesus was speaking from another dimension. He was subduing one reality with another reality. This is in essence the conversion of two spiritual forces—the prophetic anointing and the spirit of faith, which are married together and function as forces in the kingdom of God.

Faith sees the thing as finished! Faith aggressively demands that the promises of God be fulfilled. Faith pleases God. It is important to note that anytime you please God, you will receive from Him.

From the days of John the Baptist until now, the kingdom of heaven has forcefully advanced, and the strong take it by force.

—MATTHEW 11:12, MEV

> And without faith it is impossible to please God, for he who comes to God must believe that He exists and that He is a rewarder of those who diligently seek Him.
>
> —Hebrews 11:6, mev

> For we walk by faith, not by sight.
>
> —2 Corinthians 5:7, mev

The prophetic anointing operates in a dimension that is not bound by earthly time or limits. It functions in the unlimited, all-knowing nature of God. Prophets and prophetic people speak that which has been revealed by the mouth and mind of God. By faith they see a thing before it manifests, and they pull it into the earth realm. Think of Elijah and the rain (1 Kings 18). He saw it, he spoke it, and he birthed it.

Jesus saw into a space beyond physical death. He was in a realm where grieving was not the ultimate reality. He had to shift the current space to align with the reality of the spirit realm. He was simply speaking forth what He saw.

This is the convergence of faith and the prophetic in action. It is the ability to see into another reality, to subdue that which is in the earth realm by that which is known in the heavenly realm. What was the result? The girl was raised from the dead! The natural dimension was swallowed up by the miracle dimension. The word of the Lord canceled the plans of hell!

I remember a time when a family came to me at the altar while I was ministering to the sick. They shared a very negative report that had been given to their loved one. As they spoke, I began to loudly proclaim, "No, no, no...heaven says no!" It burst forth from my spirit with an uncommon velocity and intensity. I just *knew* what God was saying.

I broke free from the realm that I was standing in and even the words that I was speaking. I spoke from another space and dimension. I spoke outside of my own human mind. My lips were overtaken with heaven's decree and plan. The miracle power of God began to flow, and healing came forth. The healing came because I was not moved by what I heard in the natural realm. The natural reality was overtaken by the reality of the spirit realm. God totally healed that child by His power and glory! Healing came because we bypassed the earth realm and cooperated with the heavenly realm. This is vital in the administration of the miraculous.

BRINGING THE MIRACLE REALM INTO THE EARTHLY REALM

Webster's definition of the word *miracle* is "an extraordinary event manifesting divine intervention in human affairs."[1] Miracles should not be uncommon in the ekklesia but a common, regular occurrence. Miracles are the fruit and evidence of our position in the kingdom.

There are several gateways that bring the miracle realm into the earthly realm:

- **Faith**: This is one of the strongest and most consistent gateways. As we partner with the word of the Lord and stand in faith, we crack open the miracle realm.

- **Acts of obedience**: When the Lord stirs our hearts to action, and we move, kingdom results are unlocked. This was the case with the four lepers who decided to take action in 2 Kings 7:3, asking, "Why do we sit here until we die?"

- **Angelic assistance**: Psalm 34:7 tells us, "The angel of the LORD encamps around those who fear Him, and rescues them." Angels of the Lord are on assignment to minister to the people of God. In 2 Kings

6:17 Elisha prayed for his servant to see the armies of angels surrounding the city. When God opened Elisha's eyes, he saw the angel armies! God also sent an angel to assist Daniel in the lion's den by shutting the mouths of the lions, working a miracle of protection and deliverance (Dan. 6:22).[2]

+ **Decrees**: Speak the Word only.

+ **Atmospheres**: Set the atmosphere and tone for the miraculous to take place.

+ **Impartations**: Impartations, such as prayer cloths, can serve as gateways to the miraculous (Rom. 1:11; Acts 19:11–12).

+ **Gifts of the Spirit**: The gifts of the Spirit, including prophecy, the word of wisdom, the working of miracles, and the gifts of healing and faith, have the ability to open heavenly realms. (See 1 Corinthians 12.)

CULTIVATING THE MIRACLE REALM

The working of miracles, one of the gifts of the Spirit listed in 1 Corinthians 12 and mentioned above, involves human participation in divine plans. There is typically a leading, an instruction, or an action, and then a kingdom explosion! We see this in the story of Jesus healing a deaf man:

> Again He went out from the region of Tyre, and came through Sidon to the Sea of Galilee, within the region of Decapolis. They brought to Him one who was deaf and spoke with difficulty, and they implored Him to lay His hand on him. Jesus took him aside from the crowd, by himself, and put His fingers into his ears, and after spitting, He touched his tongue with the saliva; and looking up to heaven with a deep sigh, He said to him, "Ephphatha!" that is, "Be opened!" And his ears were opened, and the impediment of his tongue was removed, and he began speaking plainly. And He gave them orders not to tell anyone; but the more He ordered them, the more widely they continued to proclaim it. They were utterly astonished, saying, "He has done all things well; He makes even the deaf to hear and the mute to speak."
>
> —MARK 7:31–37

As Jesus ministered to the man, He did something unusual. The working of miracles will often require unusual action. Don't ask God for the gift of the working of miracles and not be willing to do things that make no sense. You will have to step out of your comfort zone and be daring. You will have to do something that may be scary and unusual.

The prayer was not lengthy. It was not seeking. It was commanding. Kingdom authority accesses kingdom miracles!

The following are some ways we can cultivate the miracle realm:

- **Pursuit**—prayer, confession, activation

- **Impartation**—one-on-one impartation, listening to teaching, reading books, catching it in the spirit

- **Inspiration**—gleaning from others, reading accounts, watching videos; when you hear and see, you will be strengthened to believe

- **Creating a consistent supernatural life**—plant yourself in the supernatural; let it become completely normal for you to hear and obey, and to expect to see results from heaven

We must be taken out of the ordinary. We must be brought into the extraordinary. We must live in a glorious position, over the flesh and the devil, and everything of the world. God has ordained us, clothed us within, and manifested upon us His glory that we may be the sons with promise, of Son-likeness to Him.[3]

—Smith Wigglesworth

If you are walking with Jesus, in the Spirit, you need not fear going too far. No believer has gone as far as God wants him to go.[4]

—A. A. Allen

The world called me a fool for having given my entire life to One whom I've never seen. I know exactly what I'm going to say when I stand in His presence. When I look upon that wonderful face of Jesus, I'll have just one thing to say: "I tried," I gave of myself the best I knew how. My redemption will have been perfected when I stand and see Him who made it all possible.[5]

—Kathryn Kuhlman

Yes, sin, sickness and disease, spiritual death, poverty and everything else that's of the devil once ruled us. But now, bless God, we rule them—for this is the Day of Dominion.[6]

—Kenneth E. Hagin

I don't base my believing on feelings. My believing is based on Your Word![7]

—Norvel Hayes

There are many wells today, but they are dry. There are many hungry souls today that are empty. But let us come to Jesus and take Him at His Word and we will find wells of salvation, and be able to draw waters out of the well of salvation, for Jesus is that well.[8]

—William J. Seymour

It's for your good! You have no business being sick—everyone of you should get well and get up and go to work, huh? Get up and go to work and earn some money and help send the gospel out! Amen![9]

—Aimee Semple McPherson

When the devil starts messing, God starts blessing.[10]

—R. W. Schambach

Your faith begins to move, to act, when the power of God supernaturally empties you of doubt and fills you with a knowing. You come into a state of knowing that you know that you know. In that instant you cannot doubt![11]

—ORAL ROBERTS

Jesus can heal anything, anywhere, anytime, and anybody. All you have to do is put your faith in Him.[12]

—JACK COE

Chapter 7

CREATING THE ATMOSPHERE

Each realm has an atmosphere, a residue. When we enter a realm, we experience the climate and culture of that particular realm. This is one of the keys to creating places of power and victory—cultivating a culture that matches the realm for which we are pressing. This happens by prayer, by revelation, by sound, and by sight.

God created the heavens and the earth as the Holy Spirit hovered upon the face of the deep. There was an atmosphere of glory out of which divine order and creativity flowed. Atmospheres produce tangible results. Spheres are set places of influence and authority. You cannot control what happens in another sphere, but you can control the atmosphere and sphere around you.

What would it look like if you purified the atmosphere and restricted negative influence from coming into your sphere? Contaminated spheres and atmospheres hinder and bind, but pure spheres and atmospheres release power, creativity, miracles, and breakthrough. Limit the negative influences in your sphere. Draw strong boundaries and close the doors to the voice of the enemy.

One definition of *atmosphere* is "a surrounding influence or environment."[1] Atmospheres are realms of creativity. Things are birthed, released, stirred, and deposited in atmospheres.

Attitudes, and the expression of those attitudes, set the emotional temperature of an atmosphere just like a thermostat sets a natural temperature. Sights and sounds help create atmospheres. Changing the sights and sounds around you can change your atmosphere.

Consider this well-known passage of Scripture:

> In the beginning God created the heavens and the earth. The earth was formless and void, and darkness was over the surface of the deep, and the Spirit of God was moving over the surface of the waters. Then God said, "Let there be light"; and there was light. God saw that the light was good; and God separated the light from the darkness. God called the light day, and the darkness He called night. And there was evening and there was morning, one day.
>
> —GENESIS 1:1–5

God released creative power! He brought forth an atmosphere of creativity and power. He created the heavens and the earth. He made everything that is seen and even that which is unseen. The earth that is described in Genesis was filled with darkness and disorder until God's power and light broke through and created something majestic out of the chaos. His Spirit brooded like a bird above the abyss.

> God spoke: "Light!" And light appeared. God saw that light was good and separated light from dark. God named the light Day, he named the dark Night. It was evening, it was morning—Day One.
> —GENESIS 1:3–5, MSG

God's words pierced the darkness, and His power created! There are realms of creative power and glory. There are realms of renewal and refreshing. There are realms of order and jurisdiction that push back the darkness.

OPPOSITION IN THE ATMOSPHERE

There are times when prophetic people are faced with unbelief and opposition in the atmosphere. Even Jesus Himself had to deal with this issue:

> But Jesus said to them, "A prophet is not without honor except in his own country, among his own relatives, and in his own house." Now He could do no mighty work there, except that He laid His

> hands on a few sick people and healed them. And
> He marveled because of their unbelief. Then He
> went about the villages in a circuit, teaching.
>
> —MARK 6:4–6, NKJV

Jesus was anointed and empowered by God to heal the sick, raise the dead, release miracles, and do mighty works. He was a walking manifestation of the realm of power and authority. Then suddenly He was hindered.

What hindered Jesus? He walked into an atmosphere of unbelief. Unbelief is like a spiritual cancer. It is toxic and full of demonic imaginations. The atmosphere Jesus stepped into was one with no expectation, no hunger, and no faith. What happened? His gift could not operate.

He was the same Jesus with the same power, the same glory, and the same anointing, but the flow was restricted. The wrong atmosphere can hinder a supernatural flow. An atmosphere of unbelief constricts the flow of God's power.

I will never forget an experience I had a few years ago. I was ministering in another nation in a powerful atmosphere. Everywhere I went in this particular nation, there was an explosion of power and miracles. It was supernatural and full of glory.

My hosts took me high into the mountains of this nation to minister in a small rural community. I was expecting a power encounter, but as I preached, I felt fierce opposition. I began to pray for the sick, still expecting miracles, but there were none. One lady did get healed in her back, which I was thankful for, but it was a diminished flow. As I was leaving, I felt weary and discouraged. How could I have gone from such power to such limitation?

While my mind was searching for answers, the enemy was hurling a barrage of discouraging words. Then I heard the Lord speak to me about the atmosphere. He told me that the trouble was the atmosphere and the culture of that church. My host confirmed what I was hearing.

When I understood what had happened, I made a vital decision. I shook the dust off and moved on! I was not about to let that atmosphere discourage or overwhelm me. I was going to the next place to torment hell and release heaven. I was moving forward with God's agenda for that nation.

Prophetic people do not allow the weight of a heavy atmosphere to dominate their minds or their thinking. They will feel it. They may even sense, taste, or smell the heaviness because their prophetic senses will engage the atmosphere. They must make a decision to cast down and reject demonic thoughts. Cast down and reject fear. Cast down and reject heaviness. Cast down and reject bitterness. Cast down and reject unbelief. Prophetic people must learn to press through and change negative atmospheres.

After that frustrating mountain service I traveled to another location, where the power of God was explosive! I was the same me. I had the same anointing, the same revelation, and the same authority. What was different was the atmosphere. We can take comfort in the example of Jesus—if God Himself was limited by an atmosphere, then we will experience those moments too.

BUILDING AN ATMOSPHERE

Leaders need to be intentional about the atmospheres they create. We are called to build atmospheres of presence, power, and glory. We are to sing songs that invite God to move. We are called to pray prayers that invite God to move. We are called to preach and teach in a way that invites God to move. We must be extremely focused and intentional about the atmospheres we are building.

Many times our atmosphere does not match our vision. We allow other people to dominate and intimidate us into allowing something much less than what heaven has written in our hearts. We need to contend for the right atmosphere that produces power and glory.

Wrong words create negative atmospheres and quench the anointing of Holy Spirit.

> Let no foul or polluting language, nor evil word
> nor unwholesome or worthless talk [ever] come
> out of your mouth, but only such [speech] as is
> good and beneficial to the spiritual progress of
> others, as is fitting to the need and the occasion,
> that it may be a blessing and give grace (God's
> favor) to those who hear it.
>
> And do not grieve the Holy Spirit of God [do
> not offend or vex or sadden Him], by Whom
> you were sealed (marked, branded as God's own,
> secured) for the day of redemption (of final deliver-
> ance through Christ from evil and the conse-
> quences of sin).
>
> —Ephesians 4:29–30, AMPC

The words of our mouth are creative weapons. We need to speak forth the plans and heart of God with prophetic insight and authority. We need to be very quick to get out of conversations and decrees that do not partner with heaven. The precious Holy Spirit is grieved when we say things that He does not like, things that do not match with the decree of heaven.

We will feel the grieving in our inner man. We will know that something is out of balance. We will know that something is off. We will know that we must stop saying what we are saying.

Breaking Unhealthy Connections

Our associations with people lead us into atmospheres, both positive and negative. When God was bringing me out of bondage, He brought people into my life with a strong revelation of authority and deliverance. He brought people who released power and anointing into my life.

I had to cut off people who tied me to bondage. I had to break some connections and close some doors. We do not need deliverance only from demons; sometimes we need deliverance from people. You have to allow God to cut the cords of association with the wrong people.

> Do not associate with a man given to anger; or go with a hot-tempered man, or you will learn his ways and find a snare for yourself.
>
> —Proverbs 22:24–25

Associating with the wrong people will open up wrong influences in your life. When you are seeking God for freedom, you must be sensitive to His leading concerning relationships in your life.

> For even though they knew God, they did not honor Him as God or give thanks, but they became futile in their speculations, and their

foolish heart was darkened. Professing to be wise, they became fools, and exchanged the glory of the incorruptible God for an image in the form of corruptible man and of birds and four-footed animals and crawling creatures.

Therefore God gave them over in the lusts of their hearts to impurity, so that their bodies would be dishonored among them. For they exchanged the truth of God for a lie, and worshiped and served the creature rather than the Creator, who is blessed forever. Amen.

For this reason God gave them over to degrading passions; for their women exchanged the natural function for that which is unnatural, and in the same way also the men abandoned the natural function of the woman and burned in their desire toward one another, men with men committing indecent acts and receiving in their own persons the due penalty of their error.

And just as they did not see fit to acknowledge God any longer, God gave them over to a depraved [*reprobate*, KJV] mind, to do those things which are not proper, being filled with all unrighteousness, wickedness, greed, evil; full of envy, murder, strife, deceit, malice; they are gossips, slanderers, haters of God, insolent, arrogant, boastful, inventors of evil, disobedient to parents, without understanding, untrustworthy, unloving, unmerciful;

and although they know the ordinance of God,
that those who practice such things are worthy
of death, they not only do the same, but also give
hearty approval to those who practice them.

—ROMANS 1:21–32

God gave them over to a reprobate mind. The word translated "reprobate" in the King James Version is *adokimos*, which means "not standing the test, not approved; that which does not prove itself such as it ought; unfit for, unproved, spurious."[2]

As the people gave themselves over to carnal atmospheres with no repentance, sin and evil behavior became normal for them. This is the danger in living in atmospheres that defy the ways of God. You begin to lose your sense of conviction.

...by means of the hypocrisy of liars seared in
their own conscience as with a branding iron.

—1 TIMOTHY 4:2

The word translated "conscience" here is the Greek word *syneidēsis*, which means "the soul as distinguishing between what is morally good and bad, prompting to do the former and shun the latter."[3] This verse is part of a warning. It says that man's conscience can become seared as with a hot iron. Think of scar tissue forming over something that is irreparably damaged. That is the picture here. The enemy wants to sear your conscience so that you are no longer sensitive to God's conviction and His drawing away from sinful living.

A sustained atmosphere creates a climate. When we build atmospheres in our lives—both good and bad— over time we create climates. If a climate remains long term, it creates a stronghold, or a way of thinking. Every culture is reinforced by thought patterns. Strongholds, systems of thought, create culture.

What would it look like if we built places that hosted a revival culture where miracles, power encounters, and the glory of God are the norm? What would it look like to create a prayer culture where people love travail and birthing?

I believe this is on the heart of God. He is releasing kingdom-building plans now for a daring new generation of leaders to build places where a heavenly culture is the norm.

A PROPHETIC WORD

As I was praying and pondering revival in this hour, the Father began to speak to my heart about the building pattern for revival. I believe that wells of revival are being dug in nations and regions to institute enduring hubs of glory.

The New Testament is a book filled with great exploits!

Churches and regional ministries were birthed in the midst of glory. The power of God erupted through radical sons and daughters who were carrying His presence. These were not just occasional meetings but a lifestyle of glory and encounter. The apostolic anointing exploded in the Book of Acts as daring pioneers boldly advanced into new territory with total abandon and complete surrender. The spirit of faith fueled the move!

I see outpourings coming forth in this hour to unlock plans for regions. Revival will be the pioneering strategy for those on the front lines. Explosive meetings will birth strong apostolic ministries that serve as regional hubs, expanding, enlarging, and establishing the kingdom. A new breed of apostolic and prophetic pioneers is coming out of the wilderness and caves, filled with glory and carrying rich reservoirs of power. They will be entrusted to steward the move and partner with the building dimensions of heaven.

These pioneers are moving in a realm of uncommon apostolic grace! They are birthing and establishing things with supernatural success and favor. This radical company will not birth a new ministry because it's a good idea but because they have a word and a solid plan! They will birth in the midst of fire.

As God ignites fires in regions, a building grace will come upon apostolic revivalists to establish kingdom works out of the midst of the fire. Prayer and Spirit-leading are key. God is positioning and repositioning people in the flow of fire. This is not a natural work but a supernatural move! We are moving in the move, following the cloud and the fire.

The Lord is releasing His pioneers, armed with revelation, armed with authority, and mantled with glory to build epic expressions of heaven on earth. They are part of His radical reform! It is truly a new day.

I believe this radical reform will bring about changes in several areas.

Changing structure

We will witness a changing wineskin, a changing government. These builders will build new and different expressions of the kingdom of God.

Changing function

We will also see a change in how the church moves and flows. These pioneers will receive prophetic insight about the systems and flows of the wine, and the wineskin needed for the move of God.

Changing sound

As a part of this reform we will begin to see a difference in how the church worships and expresses current prophetic ministry. The new sound will match the climate and the atmosphere. There are new sounds, new songs coming forth. God is releasing prayer sounds, healing sounds, and glory sounds.

> He put a new song in my mouth, a song of praise to our God; many will see and fear and will trust in the LORD.
>
> —PSALM 40:3

> Sing to the LORD a new song; sing to the LORD, all the earth.
>
> —PSALM 96:1

> Sing to Him a new song; play skillfully with a shout of joy.
>
> —PSALM 33:3

> O sing to the LORD a new song, for He has done wonderful things, His right hand and His holy arm have gained the victory for Him.
>
> —PSALM 98:1

> Praise the LORD! Sing to the LORD a new song, and His praise in the congregation of the godly ones.
>
> —PSALM 149:1

> Sing to the LORD a new song, sing His praise
> from the end of the earth! You who go down to
> the sea, and all that is in it. You islands, and those
> who dwell on them.
>
> —ISAIAH 42:10

God will release His psalmists and minstrels to bring forth the song of the Lord. They will usher people into the new song. They will usher people into the prophetic song. Remember the song of the Lord goes out ahead!

Changing priorities

We will see a radical refocusing on first things, including our first love and first ministry. Jesus rebuked people who had left their first love. The enemy uses the cares of this world and the pride of life to distract our hearts from our first love. Our commitment to be radical, passionate Jesus-lovers is foundational.

> But I have this against you, that you have left your
> first love.
>
> —REVELATION 2:4

Second, to refocus on first ministry involves a return to worshipping and loving God. Before we ever grace a stage or engage in any public service for the Lord, we are to first worship, adore, and magnify Him in private.

Surrender is our privilege. We are born to love the Lord and be loved by Him. The strongest service flows from the deep place of abiding.

> And He said to him, "'You shall love the Lord your God with all your heart, and with all your soul, and with all your mind.' This is the great and foremost commandment."
>
> —MATTHEW 22:37–38

God is raising up places of first love and first works. He is raising up houses and ministries of extravagant worship and glory.

Chapter 8

DISCOVERING THE WISDOM OF GOD

THIS DISCOVERY OF realms and dimensions is a journey deep into the vast and mysterious wisdom of God. He is inviting us to discover who He is, the power available to us, and the mysteries of His will.

> When I gave my heart to know wisdom and to see the task which has been done on the earth (even though one should never sleep day or night), and I saw every work of God, I concluded that man cannot discover the work which has been done under the sun. Even though man should seek laboriously, he will not discover; and though the wise man should say, "I know," he cannot discover.
> —ECCLESIASTES 8:16–17

Men attempt to seek out mysteries and meaning, but they come up short. At the end of man's wisdom you come to the beginning of the wisdom of God. It is impossible for a finite man to fully comprehend and measure the totality of God's infinite wisdom. The only way to begin the journey is through the realm of the Spirit.

God opens up His wisdom to us in the realm of the Spirit as we plunge deep into Him. He is not hiding anything from us, but He has preserved these things for us to discover! Discovery is the portion of sons, one of the employments of prayer. Mysteries are unlocked through extended times of prayer and meditation in the Spirit.

> But ye, beloved, building up yourselves on your most holy faith, praying in the Holy Ghost…
>
> —JUDE 20, KJV

> For he that speaketh in an unknown tongue speaketh not unto men, but unto God, for no man understandeth him; howbeit in the spirit he speaketh mysteries.
>
> —1 CORINTHIANS 14:2, KJV

Praying in the Spirit, or in tongues, uncovers the hidden mysteries of God. As you pray in the Spirit, you leave the earthly realm and enter the realm of the Holy Ghost. You pray out the mind of God. You pray out the wisdom of God. You pray out the understanding of God. The mind of God is revealed and overtakes your human mind. You will experience sudden flashes of revelation. This is the interpretation of what you prayed out in the secret place. Praying in tongues is a vital key to stewarding dimensions of mysteries and revelation.

> Oh, the depth of the riches both of the wisdom and knowledge of God! How unsearchable are His judgments and unfathomable His ways!
>
> —ROMANS 11:33

God's wisdom and ways cannot be revealed by earthly wisdom but only by heavenly wisdom. Releasing the realm of wisdom in your life creates access to answers and solutions. It creates access to revelation and understanding.

Make a decision today that you are going to enter realms and dimensions of power and glory. Decree that you discern and steward the dimensions of God. Come to the understanding that you were born to be in this world but not of this world!

> If ye were of the world, the world would love his own: but because ye are not of the world, but I have chosen you out of the world, therefore the world hateth you.
>
> —JOHN 15:19, KJV

> Jesus answered, My kingdom is not of this world: if my kingdom were of this world, then would my

servants fight, that I should not be delivered to the Jews: but now is my kingdom not from hence.
—JOHN 18:36, KJV

And be not conformed to this world: but be ye transformed by the renewing of your mind, that ye may prove what is that good, and acceptable, and perfect, will of God.

—ROMANS 12:2, KJV

Love not the world, neither the things that are in the world. If any man love the world, the love of the Father is not in him.

—1 JOHN 2:15, KJV

I have given them thy word; and the world hath hated them, because they are not of the world, even as I am not of the world.

—JOHN 17:14, KJV

And he said unto them, Ye are from beneath; I am from above: ye are of this world; I am not of this world.

—JOHN 8:23, KJV

They are not of the world, even as I am not of the world.

—JOHN 17:16, KJV

For we wrestle not against flesh and blood, but against principalities, against powers, against the rulers of the darkness of this world, against spiritual wickedness in high places.

—EPHESIANS 6:12, KJV

For our conversation is in heaven; from whence also we look for the Saviour, the Lord Jesus Christ.

—PHILIPPIANS 3:20, KJV

Set your affection on things above, not on things on the earth.

—COLOSSIANS 3:2, KJV

We are multidimensional people. We are presently living in this natural realm, but our spirit man is not of this earth. We represent another realm and dimension. We can invade this earth realm with the power and glory of God. We can be in two places at once in the spiritual sense. We are not bound by time and elements, because our spirit man is seated in Christ above the forces of the earth.

We exercise dominion and authority as multidimensional people. We speak the Word of God with power and conviction. We pray prayers of faith and breakthrough by the Spirit of the Lord!

DECREES

I walk in the glory realm.

I expect to see the manifest glory of God everywhere that I go.

I expect to see the cloud and the fire everywhere that I go.

I am uncommon because I am not born of this world; I am born of God.

I walk in the miracle realm.

I experience signs, wonders, and miracles.

I expect the supernatural and the impossible to manifest.

I expect miracles in my life.

I expect healing miracles.

I expect financial miracles.

I expect family miracles.

I decree and declare the miracle realm will operate in my life.

I move in the prophetic realm.

I supernaturally know the mysteries of God.

My spiritual eyes see.

My spiritual ears hear.

My spiritual mind knows.

I am led by the Spirit of God.

I move in the supernatural realms of God.

I decree that I rightly discern realms and dimensions to manifest the kingdom of God.

I break limitation off my life. I break limitation off my thoughts. I do not think limited. I do not dream limited. I do not pray limited. I move in the realm of the unlimited. I move in the power realm. I move in the glory realm. I move in the realm of faith. I move in the heavenly realms. I am guided and directed by the Almighty. I am rightly positioned in the timing and will of God.

I am a glory carrier in the mighty name of Jesus. Amen.

NOTES

CHAPTER 1: DIMENSIONS AND REALMS

1. "History of John G. Lake," Healing Rooms Ministries, accessed March 14, 2019, http://healingrooms.com/index .php?page_id=422.

2. John G. Lake, *Your Power in the Holy Spirit*, comp. Roberts Liardon (New Kensington, PA: Whitaker House, 2010), 296.

3. Bible Hub, s.v. *"epouranios,"* accessed March 14, 2019, https://biblehub.com/greek/2032.htm.

4. John G. Lake, *Adventures In God* (n.p., GodSounds, 2016), 8.

CHAPTER 2: PROPHETIC REALMS

1. Bill Johnson, *Dreaming With God* (Shippensburg, PA: Destiny Image, 2006), 60, 66.

CHAPTER 5: THE GLORY REALM

1. Ruth Ward Heflin, *Revival Glory* (Hagerstown, MD: McDougal, 1998), 190.

2. See "Joshua Mills Quotes," The Zedekiah List, accessed March 14, 2019, https://www.zedekiahlist.com/cgi -bin/quotes.pl?&id=5502022.

Chapter 6: The Miracle Realm

1. *Merriam-Webster*, s.v. "miracle," accessed March 14, 2019, https://www.merriam-webster.com/dictionary/miracle.

2. For more information about God sending His angels, see Debbie McDaniel's article "Five (Biblical) Reasons Why God Might Send His Angels," accessed March 15, 2019, https://www.crosswalk.com/faith/spiritual-life/5-biblical -reasons-why-god-might-send-his-angels.html?.

3. Smith Wigglesworth, *Smith Wigglesworth on Prayer*, comp. Roberts Liardon (Shippensburg, PA: Destiny Image, 2005), https://books.google.com/books?id=LR2k3ieE9_QC&p.

4. A. A. Allen, *The Price of God's Miracle Working Power* (Lamar, CO: A. A. Allen, 1950).

5. Roberts Liardon, *Kathryn Kuhlman: A Spiritual Biography of God's Miracle Worker* (New Kensington, PA: Whitaker House, 2005), https://books.google.com /books?id=fiP2BgAAQBAJ&pg.

6. Kenneth E. Hagin, "Rejoice! This Is The Day Which The Lord Hath Made!," Apostolic Information Service, August 22, 2008, https://www.apostolic.edu/rejoice-this-is-the-day -which-the-lord-hath-made/.

7. Norvel Hayes, *Why You Should Speak in Tongues* (Tulsa, OK: Harrison House, 1982), https://www.amazon.com /Why-You-Should-Speak-Tongues/dp/0892742445.

8. Vinson Synan and Charles R. Fox Jr., *William J. Seymour: Pioneer of the Azusa Street Revival* (Alachua, FL: Bridge-Logos, 2012), https://books.google.com/books ?id=fclRXXdLZc0C&pg.

9.   Sandra J. Sarkela, Susan Ross, and Margaret Lowe, *From Megaphones to Microphones: Speeches of American Women, 1920–1960* (Westport, CT: Praeger, 2003), https://www.amazon.com/Megaphones-Microphones-Speeches-American-1920-1960/dp/0275977722.

10.   Ann Spangler and Shari MacDonald, *Don't Stop Laughing Now!* (Grand Rapids, MI: Zondervan, 2002), chapter 14, https://books.google.com/books?id=hHPXDQAAQBAJ&pg.

11.   Oral Roberts, *When You See the Invisible, You Can Do the Impossible* (Shippensburg, PA: Destiny Image, 2002), 67, https://books.google.com/books?id=cc5KPpjPsNAC&pg.

12.   *Heroes of Faith* (Tulsa, OK: Harrison House, 1996), https://books.google.com/books?id=ckmjL8VHI0kC&q.

CHAPTER 7: CREATING THE ATMOSPHERE

1.   *Merriam-Webster*, s.v. "atmosphere," accessed March 14, 2019, https://www.merriam-webster.com/dictionary/atmosphere.

2.   Blue Letter Bible, s.v. *"adokimos,"* accessed March 14, 2019, https://www.blueletterbible.org/lang/lexicon/lexicon.cfm?t=kjv&strongs=g96.

3.   Blue Letter Bible, s.v. *"syneidēsis,"* accessed March 14, 2019, https://www.blueletterbible.org/lang/lexicon/lexicon.cfm?Strongs=G4893&t=KJV.